# GABRIEL JACKSON

# TO THE FIELD OF STARS

SATB, violoncello, 2 percussion

SCORE

MUSIC DEPARTMENT

OXFORD
UNIVERSITY PRESS

*To the Field of Stars* was jointly commissioned by Melbourne Symphony Orchestra Chorus, Nederlands Kamerkoor, and St Jacob's Chamber Choir, Stockholm, to commemorate the 400th anniversary of the death of Tomas Luis de Victoria and the pilgrimages to Santiago de Compostela.

The first performance was given by Melbourne Symphony Orchestra Chorus, with Sharon Draper (cello), directed by Jonathan Grieves-Smith, on 19 November 2011 at Sacred Heart Cathedral, Bendigo, Australia.

## CONTENTS

## INSTRUMENTATION

PERCUSSION 1:   7 HANDBELLS
                CROTALES

PERCUSSION 2:   TUBULAR BELL
                GLOCKENSPIEL

VIOLONCELLO

**Note:**

PERCUSSION 1 SHOULD BE TO THE LEFT AND PERCUSSION 2 TO THE RIGHT OF THE CHOIR, WITH THE VIOLONCELLO IN FRONT IN THE CENTRE. THE CELLO MAY BE DISCREETLY AMPLIFIED IF IT IS NECESSARY TO DO SO TO ACHIEVE AN IDEAL BALANCE.

Duration: *c.* 34 minutes

# TEXTS

## INTRADA

| | |
|---|---|
| Primus ex apostolis, | *First among apostles,* |
| Martir Ierosolimis, | *martyr in Jerusalem* |
| Iacobus egregio | *James is made holy* |
| Sacer est martirio. | *by his extraordinary martyrdom.* |

## REFRAIN

| | |
|---|---|
| Dum pater familias, | *When God the Father,* |
| Rex universorum, | *universal King,* |
| Donaret provincias | *bestowed each apostle authority* |
| Ius apostolorum, | *over an earthly province,* |
| Iacobus Hispanias | *James, shining light of virtue* |
| Lux illustrat morum. | *was chosen to enlighten Spain.* |

*from the* Codex Calixtinus

## 1. PRAYER FOR TRAVELLING

Life be in my speech,
Sense in what I say,
The bloom of cherries on my lips,
Till I come back again.

The love Christ Jesus gave
Be filling every heart for me,
The love Christ Jesus gave
Filling me for every one.

Traversing corries, traversing forests,
Traversing valleys long and wild.
The fair white Mary still uphold me,
The Shepherd Jesu be my shield,
The fair white Mary still uphold me,
The Shepherd Jesu be my shield.

*from* Carmina Gadelica
Translation by Alexander Carmichael (1832-1912)

## REFRAIN

| | |
|---|---|
| Iacobi Gallecia | *Galicia asks for* |
| Opem rogat piam, | *the merciful aid of James,* |
| Glebe cuius Gloria | *his Glory illuminates* |
| Dat insignem viam, | *the earthly road* |
| Ut precum frequentia | *that the crowd may sing* |
| Cantet melodiam. | *songs of praise.* |

## 2. PILGRIMS' SONG WITH HISTORY LESSON

Herru Santiagu,
Got Santiagu,
E ultreia, e suseia,
Deus adiuva nos.

I have always regretted that We could not find time to make a Pilgrimage to Saint Iago de Compostella. We were informed, particularly by Mr. Lagoanere, that the Original of this Shrine and Temple of St. Iago was this. A certain Shepherd saw a bright Light there in the night. Afterwards it was revealed to an Archbishop that St. James was buried there. This laid the Foundation of a Church, and they have built an Altar on the Spot where the Shepherd saw the Light. In the time of the Moors, the People made a Vow, that if the Moors should be driven from this Country, they would give a certain portion of the Income of their Lands to Saint James. The Moors were defeated and expelled and it was reported and believed, that Saint James was in the Battle and fought with a drawn Sword at the head of the Spanish Troops, on Horseback. The People, believing that they owed the Victory to the Saint, very cheerfully fulfilled their Vows by paying the Tribute.

Upon the Supposition that this is the place of the Sepulture of Saint James, there are great numbers of Pilgrims, who visit it, every Year, from France, Spain, Italy and other parts of Europe, many of them on foot.

Saint Iago is called the Capital of Gallicia, because it is the Seat of the Archbishop and because Saint James is its Patron.

John Adams (1735-1826)

## REFRAIN

| | |
|---|---|
| Iacobo dat parium | *The whole of mankind* |
| Omnis mundus gratis, | *freely gives thanks to James,* |
| Ob cuius remedium | *soldier of piety;* |
| Miles pietatis | *through his help* |
| Cunctorum presidium | *he redeems all, answering* |
| Est ad vota satis. | *our prayers.* |

## 3. WALKING WITH GOD

Oh! for a closer walk with God,
   A calm and heavenly frame;
A light to shine upon the road
   That leads me to the Lamb!

Where is the blessedness I knew
   When first I saw the Lord?
Where is the soul-refreshing view
   Of Jesus and his word?

What peaceful hours I once enjoyed!
   How sweet their memory still!
But they have left an aching void,
   The world can never fill.

Return, O holy Dove, return,
   Sweet messenger of rest;
I hate the sins that made thee mourn,
   And drove thee from my breast.

The dearest idol I have known,
   Whate'er that idol be;
Help me to tear it from thy throne,
   And worship only thee.

So shall my walk be close with God,
   Calm and serene my frame;
So purer light shall mark the road
   That leads me to the Lamb.

William Cowper (1731-1800)

## REFRAIN

| | |
|---|---|
| Iacobum miraculis | *By the miracles* |
| Que fiunt per illum. | *that James accomplishes* |
| Arctis in periculis | *in the straits of danger* |

Acclamet ad illum,
Quisquis solvi vinculis
Sperat propter illum.

*let whoever hopes*
*to be freed from his bonds*
*cry out to him.*

## 4. MIRACLES

Why, who makes much of a miracle?
As to me I know of nothing else but miracles,
Whether I walk the streets of Manhattan,
Or dart my sight over the roofs of houses toward the sky,
Or wade with naked feet along the beach just in the edge of
the water,
Or stand under trees in the woods,
Or talk by day with any one I love, or sleep in the bed at night
with any one I love,
Or sit at table at dinner with the rest,
Or look at strangers opposite me riding in the car,
Or watch honey-bees busy around the hive of a summer
forenoon,
Or animals feeding in the fields,
Or birds, or the wonderfulness of insects in the air,
Or the wonderfulness of the sundown, or of stars shining so
quiet and bright,
Or the exquisite delicate thin curve of the new moon in
spring;
These with the rest, one and all, are to me miracles,
The whole referring, yet each distinct and in its place.

Walt Whitman (1819-1892)

## REFRAIN

O beate Iacobe,
Virtus nostra vere,
Nobis hostes remove
Tuos ac tuere
Ac devotos adhibe
Nos tibi placere.

*O blessed James*
*truly our strength,*
*take our enemies from us*
*and protect your people*
*and enable us your devotees*
*to please you.*

## 5. OUR JOUNEY HAD ADVANCED

Our journey had advanced;
Our feet were almost come
To that odd fork in Being's road,
Eternity by term.

Our pace took sudden awe,
Our feet reluctant led.
Before were cities, but between,
The forest of the dead.

Retreat was out of hope,
Behind, a sealed route,
Eternity's white flag before,
And God at every gate.

Emily Dickinson (1830-1886)

## REFRAIN

Iacobo propicio
Veniam speremus
Et, quas ex obsequio
Merito debemus
Patri tam eximio
Dignas laudes demus.
Amen.

*With James's favour,*
*let us hope for forgiveness,*
*and give the due praises*
*that we rightly owe*
*to so outstanding*
*a Father*
*Amen.*

## 6. CAMPUS STELLAE (THE FIELD OF STARS)

Aldebaran. Gorgonea Tertia. Minelava. Torcularis Septentrionalis. Betelgeuse. Hydrobius. Nair Al Saif. Ushakaron. Canopus. Izar. Okul. Vindemiatrix. Decrux. Jabbah. Polaris Australis. Wasat. Etamin. Kitalpha. Rotanev. Yed Posterior. Fum al Samakah. Lucida Anseris. Sirius. Zavijava. Elmuthalleth. Kornephoros. Ras Algethi. Terrebellum. Al Minliar al Asad. Shurnakabtishashutu. Proxima Centauri. Zuben-al-Akribi. Deneb Algedi.
Miaplacidus.

Vulpecula. Andromeda. Ursa Minor. Boötes. Tucana. Camelopardalis. Sagitta. Delphinus. Reticulum. Eridanus. Perseus. Fornax. Octans. Grus. Norma. Horologium. Microscopium. Indus. Leo Minor. Monoceros. Indus. Lacerta.

Iacobe servorum spes et medicina tuorum.
Redde tuis vitam per tempora longa cupitam.
Ut superum castris iungi mereamur in astris.

*James, your servants' hope and healing, restore to your people*
*the life long yearned-for, that we may be found worthy to reach*
*the heavenly citadels among the stars.*

Antiphon at First Vespers, Feast of St James

Zaurak. Sheliak. La Superba. Formalhaut. Yildun. Rigil Kentauris. Kaffaljidhma. Eltrain. Wezen. Pulcherrima. Jih. Deneb Kaitos Schemali.
Vega. Okul. Izar. Cor Caroli. Unukalhai. Nashira. Head of Hydra. Birhan Isat. Talith Borealis. Menkalinen. Gienar Gunab. Alfecca Meridiana.

## 7. COMPOSTELA (O QUAM GLORIOSUM)

O quam gloriosum est regnum in quo cum Christo gaudent omnes sancti. Amicti stolis albis sequuntur Agnum quocumque ierit.

*O how glorious is the kingdom in which all the saints rejoice with Christ.*
*Clad in robes of white they follow the Lamb wherever he goes.*

Magnificat Antiphon at Second Vespers, Feast of All Saints

O lux et decus Hispanie, sanctissime Iacobe; qui inter apostolos primatum tenes, primus eorum martirio laureatus.
O singulare presidium, qui meruisti videre Redemptorum nostrum adhuc mortalem in deitate transformatum; exaudi preces servorum tuorum, et intercede pro nostra salute omniumque populorum.

*O light and glory of Spain, most holy James, who, pre-eminent among the apostles, was the first to be crowned with the laurels of martyrdom. O singular protector, who deservedly saw our Redeemer when, after his mortal life, he was made divine, grant the prayers of your servants, and intercede for our salvation, and that of all peoples.*

Magnificat Antiphon at Second Vespers, Feast of St James

*Commissioned by the Melbourne Symphony Orchestra Chorus, the Netherlands Chamber Choir and St Jacob's Chamber Choir, Stockholm*

# To the Field of Stars

## INTRADA

GABRIEL JACKSON

First performed by the Melbourne Symphony Orchestra Chorus with Sharon Draper (violoncello), directed by Jonathan Grieves-Smith, at the Sacred Heart Cathedral, Bendigo, on 19 November 2011

2

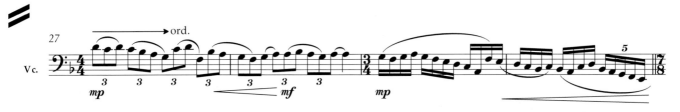

# REFRAIN

# 1. PRAYER FOR TRAVELLING

Christ___ Je - sus___ gave,___ (S.)

Christ___ Je - sus___ gave,___ Be fill - ing (A.)

Christ___ Je - sus___ gave,___ Be fill - ing (T.)

Christ___ Je - sus___ gave,___ Be fill - ing (B.)

The love___ (S.)

e - very heart___ for___ me, The love___ (A.)

e - very heart for me, The love___ (T.)

e - very heart___ for___ me, The love___ (B.)

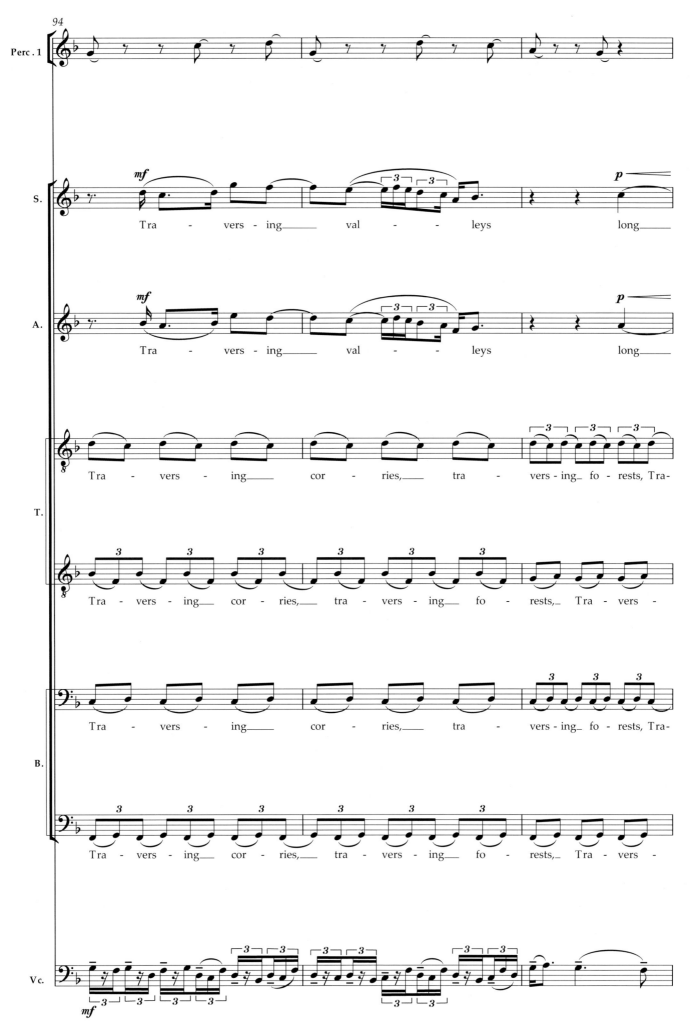

14

# REFRAIN

que - e - ti - a    Ca - an - tet____ me - lo - o - di - i - am.

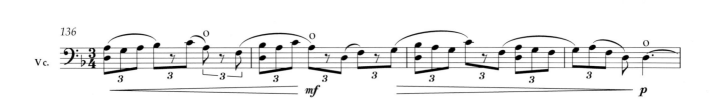

## 2. PILGRIMS' SONG WITH HISTORY LESSON

177
S.
A.
T.
Vc.
p
Her - ru San - ti - a - - - gu, Got
Her - ru San - ti - a - - - - - gu,
SOLO
spoken, clearly and firmly, in natural speech rhythm
I have always regretted that We could not find time to make a Pilgrimage to Saint Iago de Compostella. We were informed, particularly by Mr Lagoanere, that the Original of this Shrine and Temple of St Iago
p mp
180
San - ti-a - - - - - - - gu,
Got San - ti - a - - - - - - - - - gu,
was this. A certain Shepherd saw a bright Light there in the night. Afterwards it was revealed to an Archbishop that St. James was buried there. This laid the Foundation of a Church, and they have built an Altar on the Spot where the
183
mp
E ul - tre - ia, e su - se - ia, E ul - tre - ia,
E ul - tre - ia, e su - se - ia, E ul -
Shepherd saw the Light. In the time of the Moors, the People made a Vow, that if the Moors should be driven from this Country, they would give a certain portion of the Income of their Lands to Saint James. The Moors were defeated
tr

**B.** who visit it, every Year, from France, Spain, Italy and other parts of Europe, many of them on foot.

**SOLO** Saint Iago is called the Capital of Gallicia, because it is the Seat of the Archbishop and because Saint James is its Patron.

# REFRAIN

# 3. WALKING WITH GOD

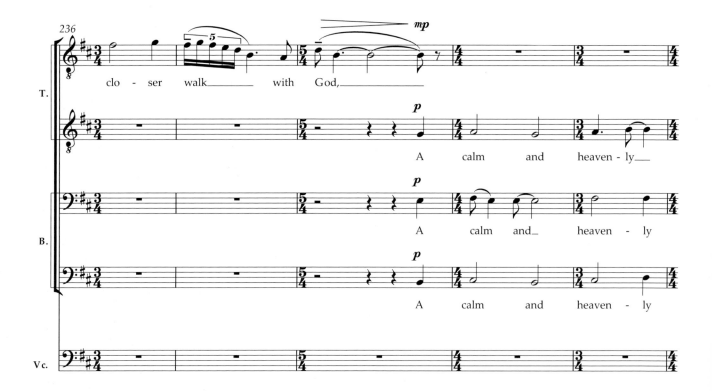

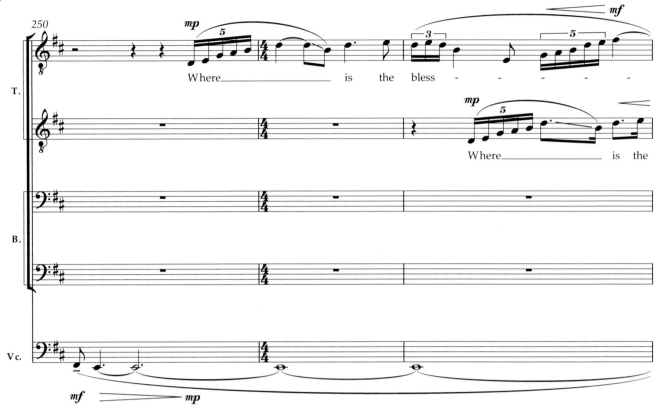

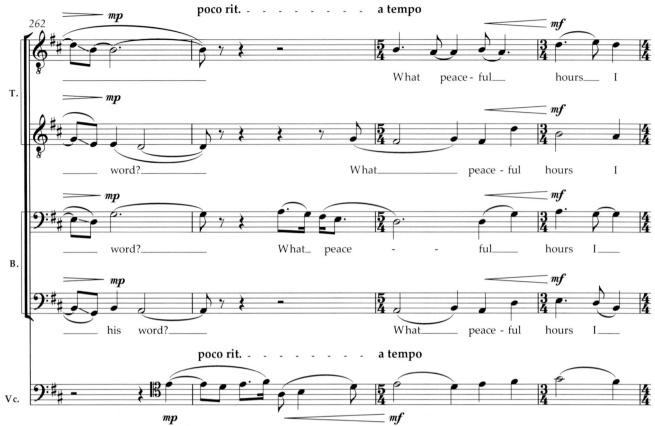

36

So pu - rer light shall mark the road That

So pu - rer light shall mark the road That

So pu - rer light shall mark the road That

So pu - rer light shall mark the road That

poco rall

leads me to the Lamb.

leads me to the Lamb.

leads me to the Lamb.

leads me to the Lamb.

poco rall

# REFRAIN

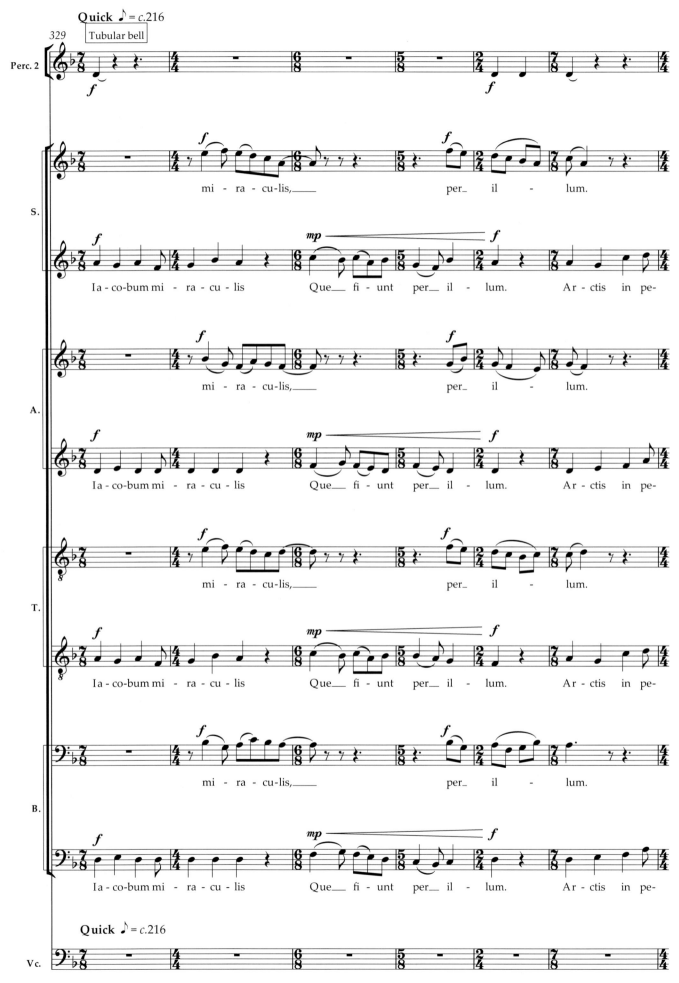

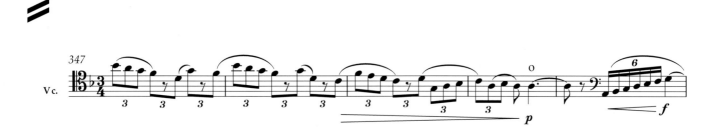

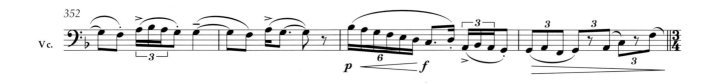

# 4. MIRACLES

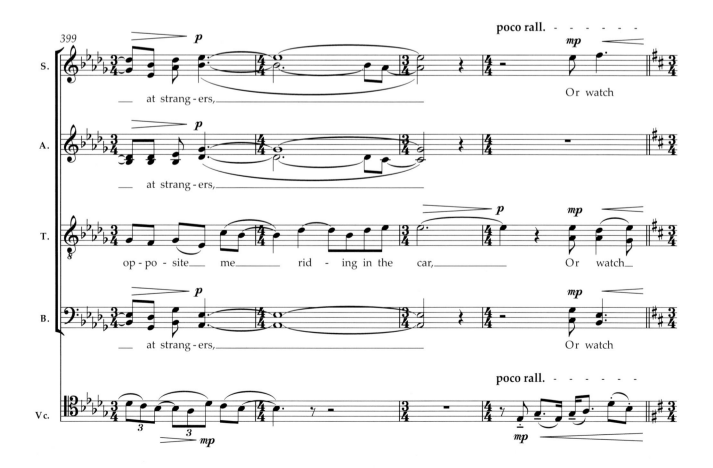

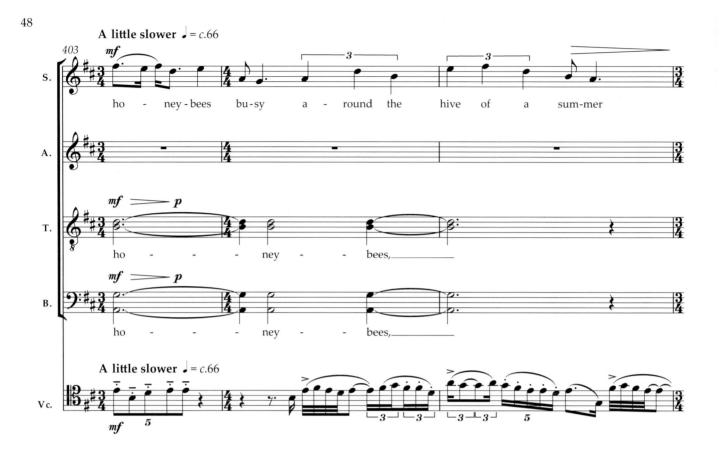

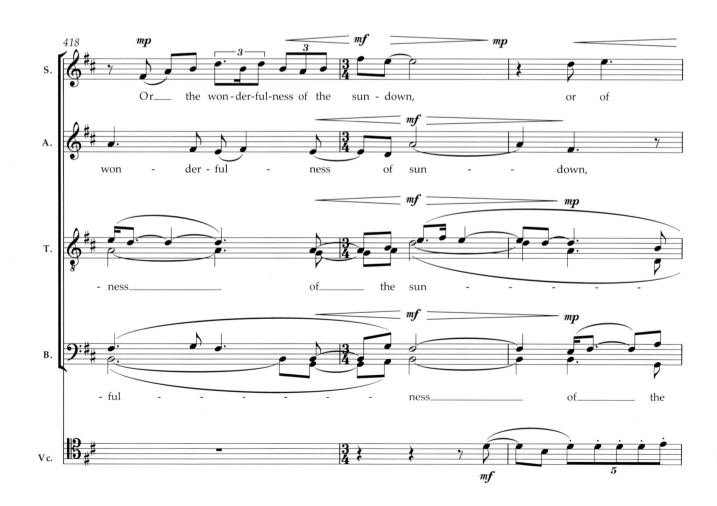

52

These with the rest, one and all, are to me mi - ra - cles,

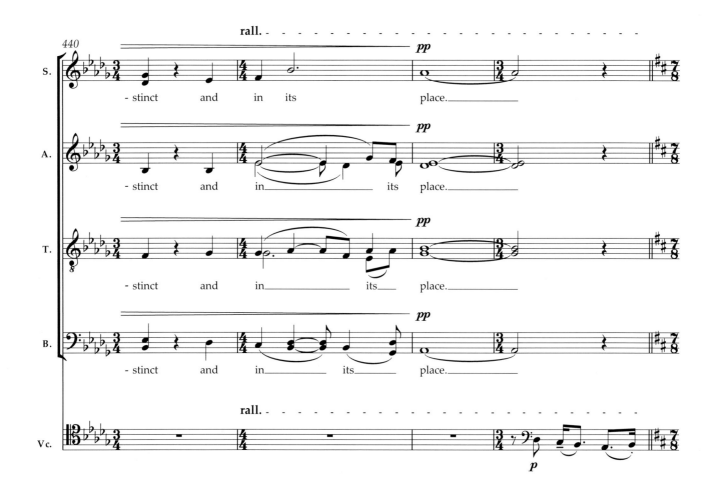

# REFRAIN

# 5. OUR JOURNEY WAS ADVANCED

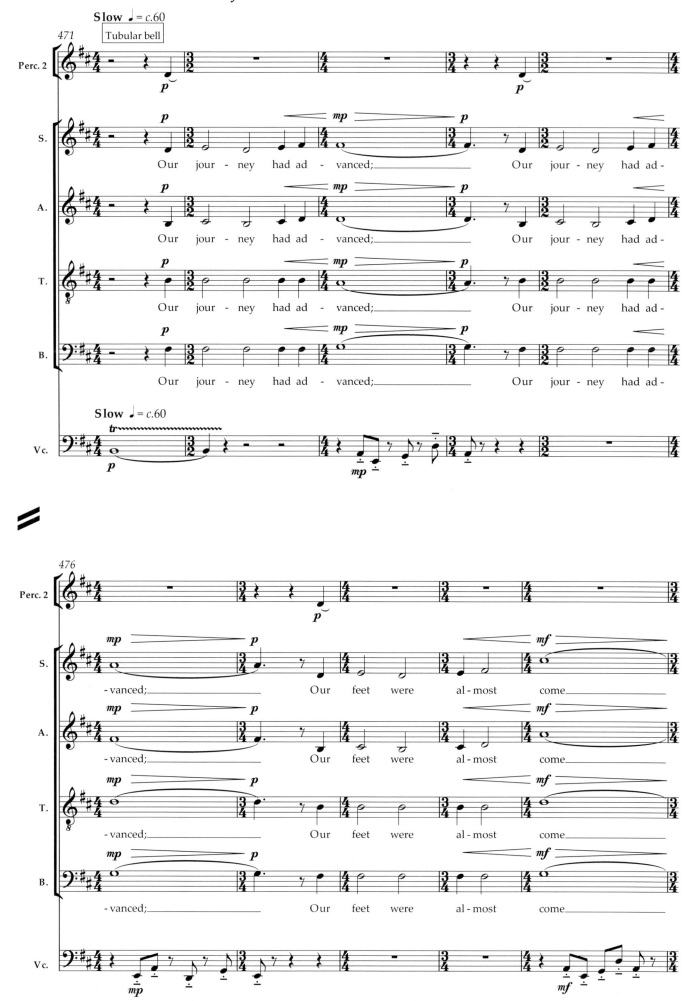

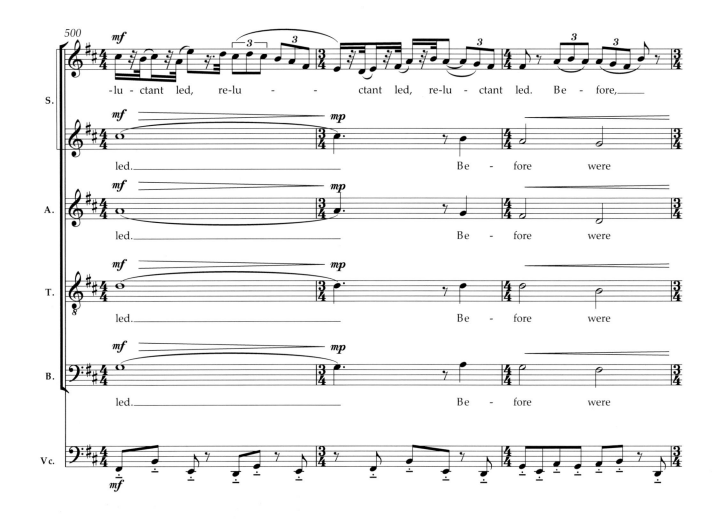

60

# REFRAIN

# 6. CAMPUS STELLAE (THE FIELD OF STARS)

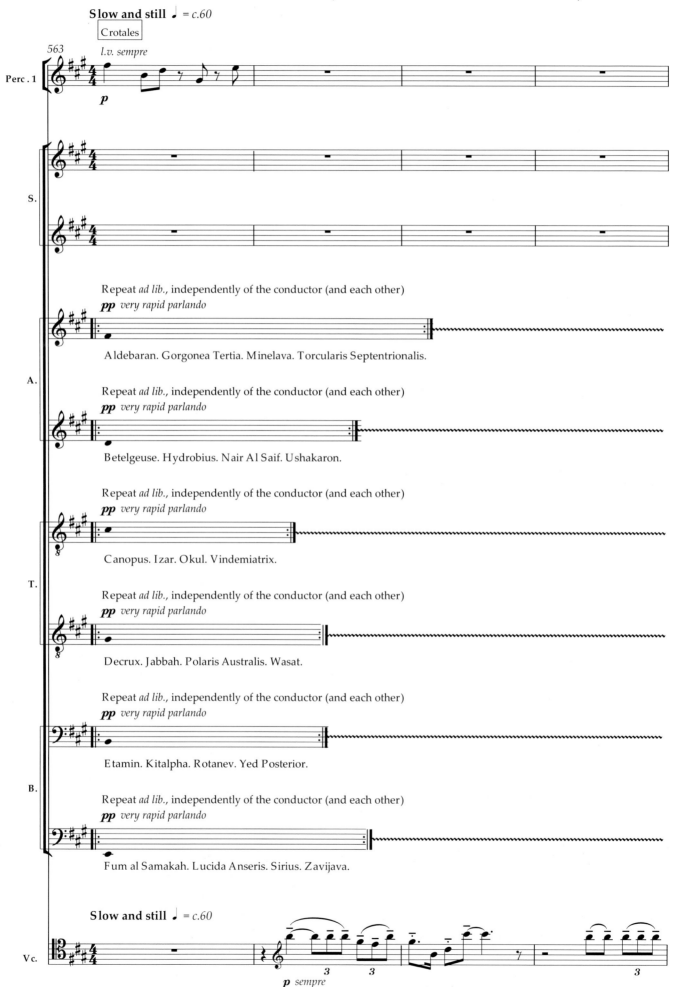

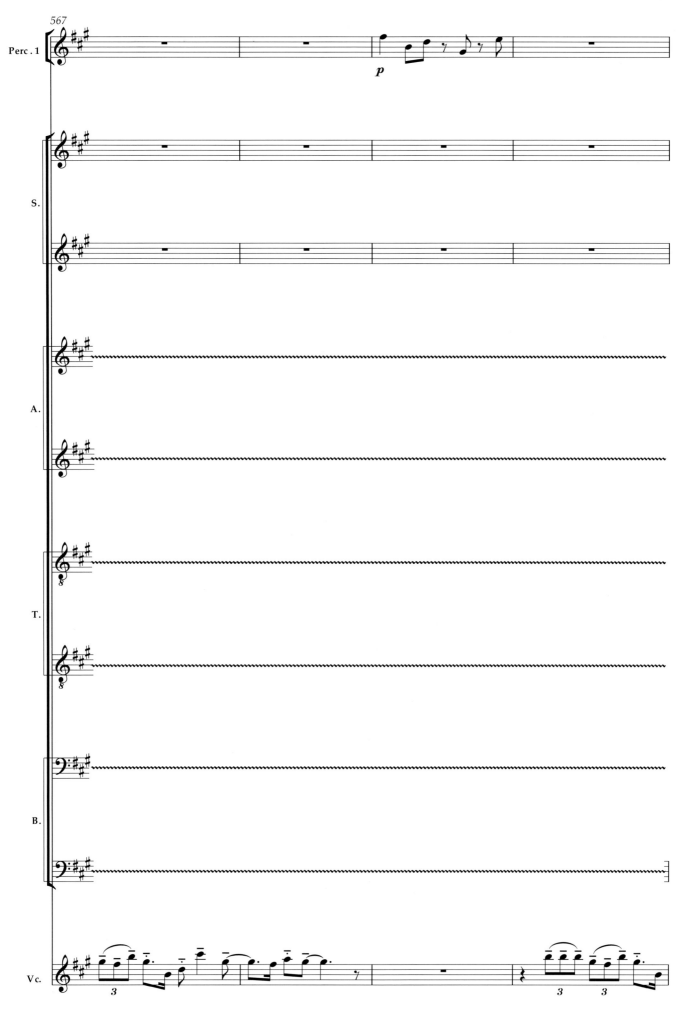

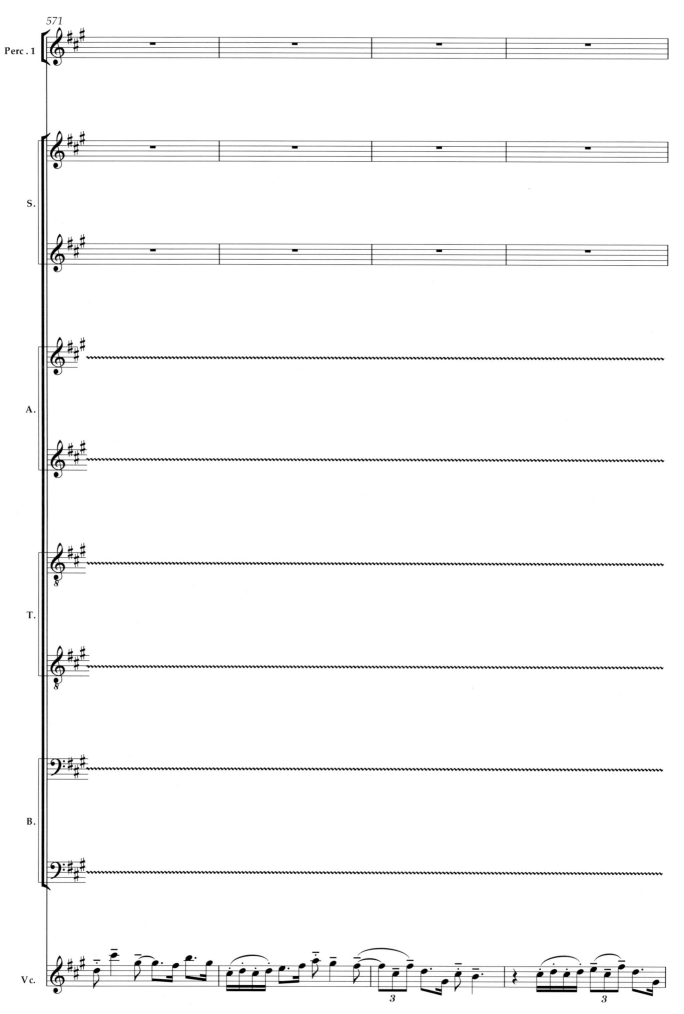

Repeat *ad lib.*, independently of the
conductor (and each other)

El - mu - tha(l) leth. Kor - ne - pho - ros.

At the conductor's signal, finish the bar you are singing
and move on immediately to the next one

Mi - a - pla - ci - dus.

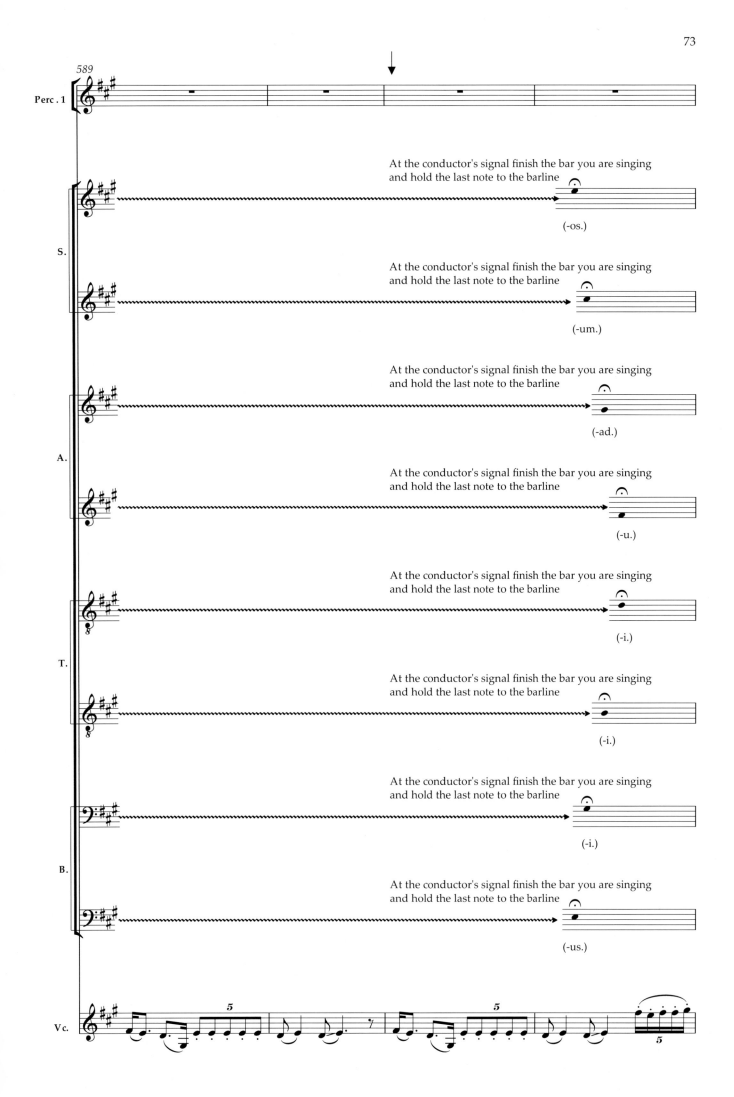

74

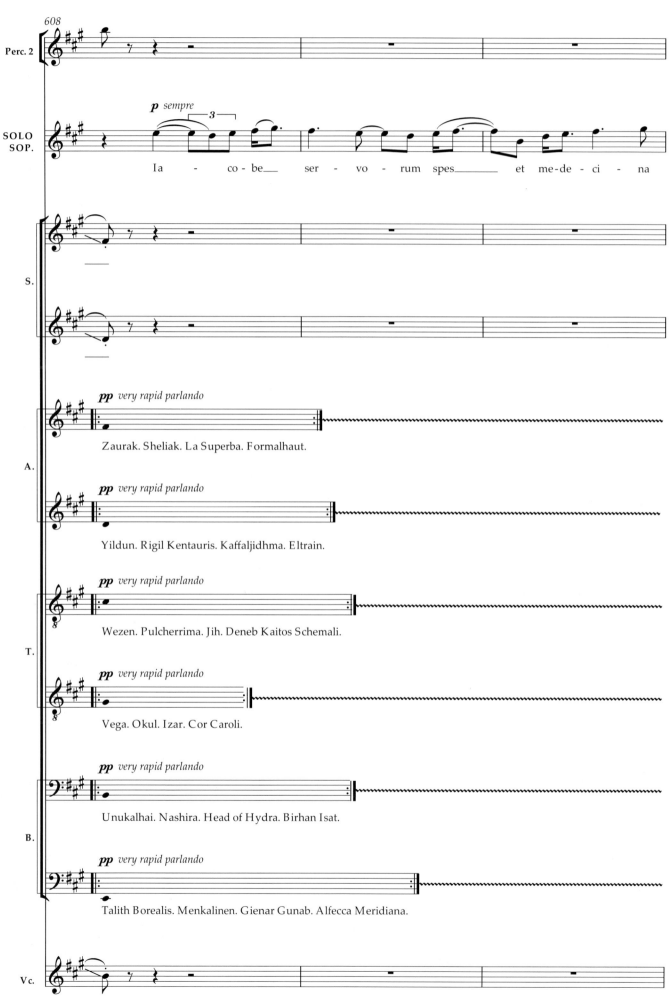

608

Perc. 2

SOLO
SOP.

*p sempre*

*3*

Ia - co - be__ ser - vo - rum spes__ et me-de - ci - na

S.

A.

**pp** *very rapid parlando*

Zaurak. Sheliak. La Superba. Formalhaut.

**pp** *very rapid parlando*

Yildun. Rigil Kentauris. Kaffaljidhma. Eltrain.

T.

**pp** *very rapid parlando*

Wezen. Pulcherrima. Jih. Deneb Kaitos Schemali.

**pp** *very rapid parlando*

Vega. Okul. Izar. Cor Caroli.

B.

**pp** *very rapid parlando*

Unukalhai. Nashira. Head of Hydra. Birhan Isat.

**pp** *very rapid parlando*

Talith Borealis. Menkalinen. Gienar Gunab. Alfecca Meridiana.

Vc.

vi - tam per__ tem - po - ra____ lon - ga____ cu - pi - tam.____

- gi me - re - a - mur___ in a - stris.

At the conductor's signal, finish the bar you singing
and hold the last note to the barline
(-aut.)

At the conductor's signal, finish the bar you singing
and hold the last note to the barline
(-ain.)

At the conductor's signal, finish the bar you singing
and hold the last note to the barline
(-i.)

At the conductor's signal, finish the bar you singing
and hold the last note to the barline
(-i.)

At the conductor's signal, finish the bar you singing
and hold the last note to the barline
(-at.)

At the conductor's signal, finish the bar you singing
and hold the last note to the barline
(-a.)

slow
trem.

# 7. COMPOSTELA (O QUAM GLORIOSUM)

88

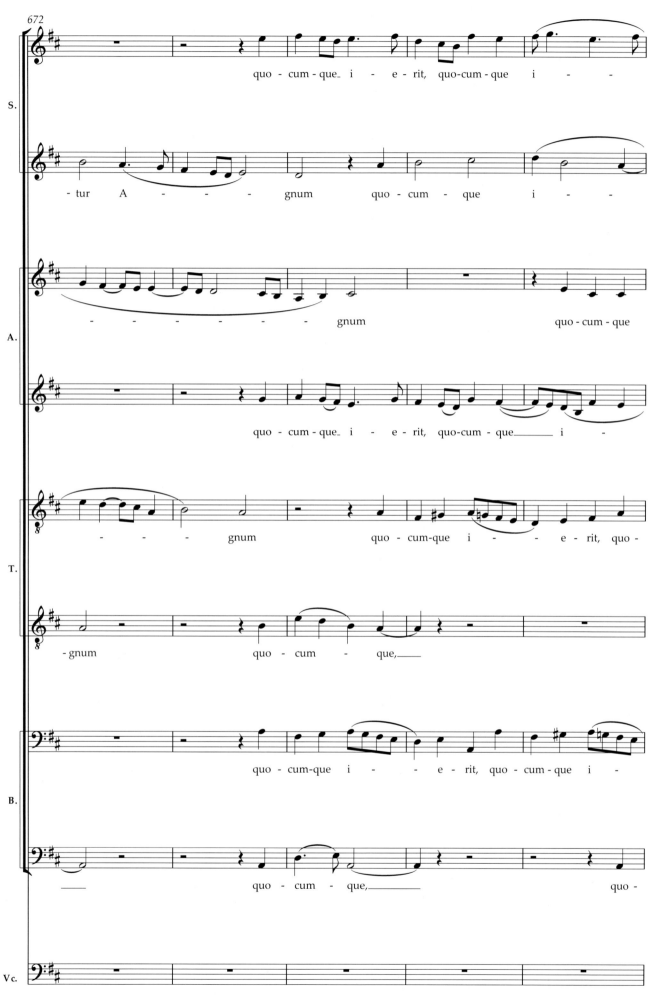

92

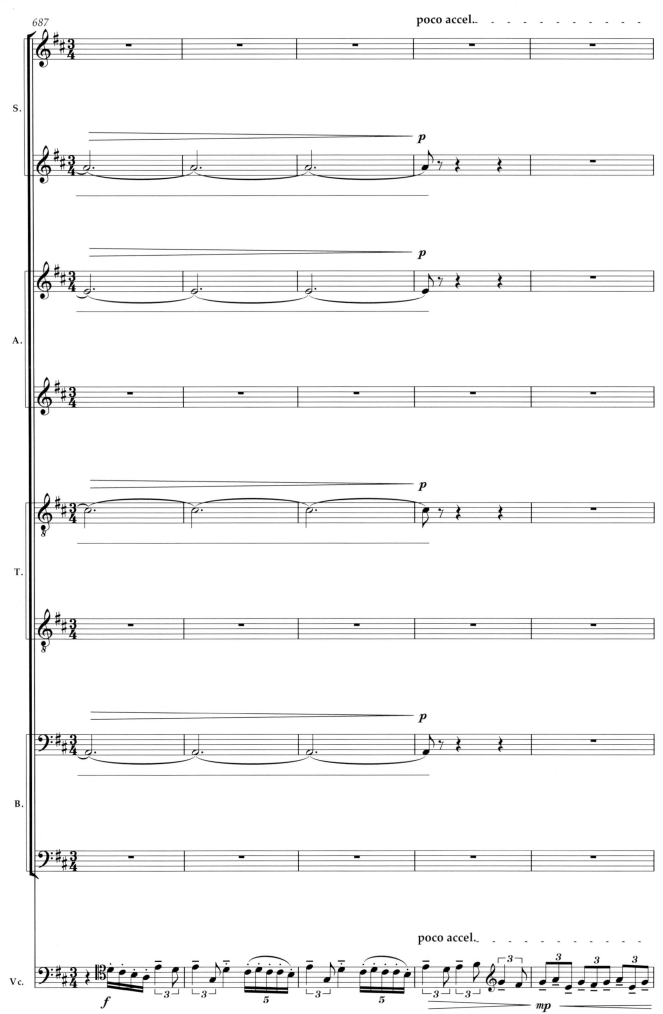

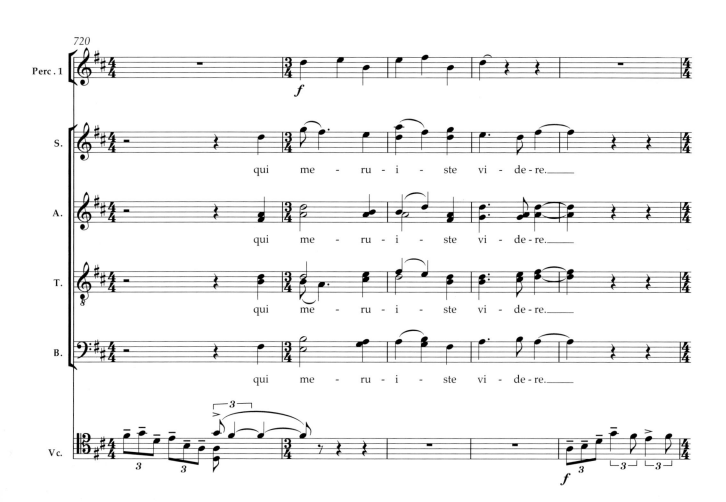

100

Brockley, October 2010-April 2011